BRB,
I Need to
Go to
Swim
Practice

a **GIRLS' GUIDE** to competition, confidence, and fun through **SWIMMING**

Luciana (Lucy) Alessi

Copyright: © 2018 by Luciana Alessi

Published by:
Decibel Trade Company
6215 Transit Road
East Amherst NY 14051

All rights reserved. No part of this book may be reproduced or transmitted in any form or by any means whatsoever without express written permission from the author, except in the case of brief quotations embodied in critical articles and reviews. Please refer all pertinent questions to the publisher.

All rights reserved. No part of this book may be reproduced or transmitted in any form or by any means, electronic or mechanical, including photocopying, recording, or by an information storage and retrieval system - except by a reviewer who may quote brief passages in a review to be printed in a magazine or newspaper - without permission in writing from the publisher.

Cover designed by Evan Stewart
Print typesetting and e-book conversion by BookCoverCafe.com
Printed in the United States of America
Library of Congress Number: 2018942298

ISNB: 978-1-7322280-0-9

Dedication

To my Mom, Dad, Brother Luca & Sister Serafina - thank you for your patience with me!

To my Grandma Rosemary, Big Daddy, Grandma Dorothy and Papa - thank you for loving me.

To all my friends, coaches and teachers - thank you for helping and believing in me.

Contents

Dedication	iii
Chapter 1 BAAC Interclub Swim Meet	**1**
How I Began Swimming	2
Chapter 2 Big Weekend: Two Meets, Twelve Events	**11**
Swimming Is About Friends	13
Chapter 3 BAAC In Action Open Meet	**17**
Swimming Is About Improving	19
Chapter 4 TTSC Halloween Meet	**21**
Swimming Is About Overcoming Disappointment	23
Chapter 5 STAR Series Meet 2	**25**
Swimming Is About Giving To Others	27
Chapter 6 BAAC to BAAC Open Meet	**29**
Swimming Is About Paying Attention To Details	30
Chapter 7 Star Series Meet 3	**31**
Swimming Is About Being Helpful	33
Chapter 8 2018 BAAC Chance Open	**35**
Swimming Is About Overcoming Challenges And Bullying	36
Chapter 9 2018 Niagara LSC Short Course Championship Qualifier	**39**
Swimming Is About Great Exercise	41
Chapter 10 Long Course Season	**45**
Swimming Future	46

Chapter 1

BAAC Interclub Swim Meet

September 16, 2017

Interclub is a smaller meet, only consisting of my swim club, and not open for invitation to outside clubs.

I was nervous, and my swimsuit was a little too tight—I must have grown over the summer. It gave me a feeling that I had weights on my shoulders. The water was cold in the UB pool early that Saturday morning. My first event was the 50m back, which I enjoyed, but it's not my best. I still have a fear of hitting my head on the wall when finishing the backstroke, which causes me to slow down at the end, hurting my time.

It was a few days before my ninth birthday, and my friend Belle and I were talking about what we should get each other for our birthdays. Belle is a year older than I am, but her birthday is on September 21 (mine is September 19). It turned out we both wanted to get each other the same present—JoJo Bows :)—colorful, oversized (what my parents say) hair bows, made popular by YouTuber JoJo Siwa.

Belle was a little nervous this morning as well. She was only nine-years-old and had to swim a 200 IM against girls who were up to five years older—one was even her babysitter! Belle swam well, but she didn't win. Swimming truly has two competitions: one against others and the other against your own best personal record.

I competed in five events for the day: 50 back, 100 IM, 100 free, 50 free, and 50 breast. Towards the end, I was getting tired and wished the order was different. The 100 IM is tiring for me, and I think it slowed my other race times down. I didn't win any events that day.

I was trying to get what's called a "B qualifying time" (It's a motivational time set forth by USA Swimming). I was the closest with two events: the 50 breast and the 50 free. I finished with a 54.75 second time for the 50 breast but needed a 53.29 time. For the 50 free, I finished with a 40.47 time but needed a 38.89 time. I was less than two seconds away with both! A fun meet, but I needed more work.

Well, back to practice with another meet four weeks out...

How I Began Swimming

I am not certain of when my love of swimming first happened. My parents remind me that I was part of a Mommy/Daddy and

CHAPTER 1: BAAC INTERCLUB SWIM MEET

me swimming program when I was five months old. I didn't love getting my face dunked in the water. However, the instructor told my parents that it was important and that "your baby will not choke." My mother was nervous about doing it to me, but my father was more than willing. So, into the water he went and under the water I went....

I had the great opportunity of living in Clarence, New York, which has a wonderful Learn to Swim Program. At the time, the director was a woman named Jamie Johnson. I loved Ms. Jamie! She made swimming fun on every Monday and Wednesday evening when I went to the pool with the other four-year-olds in level one. My father said that we looked like a bunch of bobblehead babies floating on top of the water.

By the time I was five, I remember looking forward to swim nights. I loved seeing Ms. Jamie and her assistants, which were the "big kid" high schoolers, but most of all, I loved being in the water. I remember seeing other kids crying about getting in the water and getting their head wet. For me, it was fun and I couldn't care less about splashing around. In fact, I would jump into the water even before the time for my class to begin—I couldn't wait.

The end of Clarence Learn to Swim Program in levels 8, 9, & 10 was to complete a one mile swim! Which was 66 laps. I was scared. I swam some, walked some, stopped, drank water, and swam some more. When all the other kids were out of the pool, I had 20 laps left to go. My father said it took me nearly an hour and a half to complete the swim. I didn't care. I did it (and I got the t-shirt to prove it)!!

Luciana age-5 celebrates achieving level-5 with her friend Hannah

When I was six, my parents enrolled me in the swim team at the Park Country Club. This is when I discovered the benefits of

CHAPTER 1: BAAC INTERCLUB SWIM MEET

practice. My first year, I was in lane one (the least competitive lane). However, I really loved being around the older girls (nine- & ten-year-olds) and was impressed by how fast they could swim and how well they could dive. In fact, I just watched them dive for half an hour every time. Fortunately, with hard work and practice, I continued to improve, and after my first summer, I was awarded "Most Improved Swimmer by Coach Dan". The trophy still sits in my bedroom!

Luciana age-6 celebrates most improved swimmer with coach Maddie

Swim Meets are scary, but a lot of fun. When I was younger, I was nervous about not lining up correctly, or when the horn sounded to start the race and not starting on time. Or worse—starting too early and jumping into the water before the horn sounded. Luckily, it's never happened to me yet, but I've seen it happen to other kids before, and I feel bad for them. Now, they're scary because I am nervous about not doing my best or beating my previous best time.

Some swim meets are smaller and some are huge. Most of the swim meets I am entered into are for ages 12 and under. But some are open meets 6 years to college age. There can be hundreds of swimmers and thousands of spectators. The hard part is waiting around in-between events.

Some of the larger swim meets can have 70 or more events. It's not uncommon to have to wait a few hours between them. Then, on the flip side, you can have two or three events consecutively. Most of the time between events, I'll just talk with my friends or eat. My mom usually packs me fruit, hummus, crackers and a sandwich. When I was six years old, I used to eat all the food at once. It was a terrible mistake. And after doing a few events with a tummy ache, I've learned to space out the food. My brother, Luca, still hasn't learned!

Swim Gear is, like, the coolest thing ever. I love the swimsuits, swim caps, goggles, swim bag, swim parka (to wear in-between events like a bathrobe), and towels. I am always picking out the next color design. Whenever the USAA Speedo catalog arrives at my house, I quickly thumb through it. I keep it up in my room for a few days, circling the things I want and hoping my parents will get it for me.

CHAPTER 1: BAAC INTERCLUB SWIM MEET

I am kind of particular about my goggles. I have tried many kinds, but I like the ones that are tinted. They are useful because the tint helps keep the glare of the bright overhead lights out of your eyes. It also works great when swimming outside and keeping the sun out of your eyes. The straps that go around the goggle are also important. Most goggles come with either a single or spit double rubber strap. I like the strap that is more like a bungee cord. So, I sometimes take the strap that comes with the goggles off and replace it with a bungee style strap. It seems to fit best for me and doesn't come off as easily when diving into the water.

My swim bag is a mermaid scale by Speedo. It's pretty and unique, but my friend, Amelia, has the same swim bag. It's great for all my gear: goggles, caps, earrings, change of clothes, and towel. It's bigger than the old backpack that I used to use, and it has more pockets. My friends Belle, Lauren, Kat also have Speedo bags, but in different colors. Belle's is pink and Kat's is orange and purple. I like their bags a lot.

Luca just got an orange Speedo swim bag for his birthday, complete with the dirt bag (no, I'm not calling him a name). The dirt bag is a wet swimsuit bag on the backside so you can separate your wet swimsuit from the rest of your clothes. Once, I mixed my wet bathing suit in with my dry clothes, and I had to wear a wet sweater home. I was freezing!

Swim Camps are held a few times a year, but the biggest one is over the summer. I attend the one at the state University of New York at Buffalo (UB). It's run by coach Andy Bashor, who is the women's head coach at the university. There are kids of ages 8–17 at the camp. This past summer was my first year, and I was scared and didn't know what to expect. It was four consecutive days and hundreds of swimmers from all around New York attend it. Since I was only eight, I wasn't allowed to sleep over in the dorms, but I can't wait until I can. The older girls say it was so much fun!

The camp was organized into the four main strokes: freestyle, backstroke, breaststroke, and butterfly. We were split into groups by age and ability level. It also consisted of classroom time where the coaches taught us more textbook information about the different strokes. What I really liked is that coaches would also videotape us swimming, both above and below the water. It was cool to see my strokes below the water and spot where I really needed work!

There was an eight-year-old boy who was at the camp as well. His name is Aiden and he swims for Clarence Swim Club, which is where I live, but I swim at a different club. He's a really good swimmer. It's not uncommon for him to swim against kids who are three or four years older and do very well against them. He is really good at the butterfly and raced against one of the assistant coaches who was in college. She beat him, but not by much. I found it funny when she said, "Maybe next time, kid."

I liked being at swim camp with my friends and making new ones. I also liked being at a big university. The coaches walked us around campus, and we got to go to the campus bookstore. I wanted to buy UB hoodies and games—I can't wait until I can go to college!

CHAPTER 1: BAAC INTERCLUB SWIM MEET

Lucy and coach Emma after a swim meet at Buffalo State College

Chapter 2

Big Weekend: Two Meets, Twelve Events

October 14-15, 2017

The morning of Saturday Oct. 14, I was nervous. I was heading downtown to the pool at ECC Flickinger Center to begin my swim meet. I had five events scheduled for the day, and this was my first time competing as a nine-year-old. I know that doesn't seem like it's a big deal, but groups are categorized as 8 and under and then 12 and under. This meant I had much harder competition.

My events for the day were:

- 50 back
- 50 breast

- 100 IM
- 50 free
- 50 fly

The first event of the day is always the toughest. I always feel nervous before I begin, like I'm not going to win or even do well at all. But once the buzzer sounds off and I jump into the water, or push off the wall, the feeling dissolves away. I instantly feel energetic and focused on my stroke. I was a little slow with my backstroke start, and within the first few seconds, already a few strokes behind my competition. I focused on my breathing and tried to move fast. I felt that at the halfway mark, my flip turn was good. I tried as hard as I could to close the gap and to finish strong. My time was 49.12 seconds. This beat my previous best of 50.96, a decrease of 1.84 seconds. Good, but not good enough. I finished 8 out of 14 girls in my event.

The second event was the 50 breast. Usually my best event; however, I was disqualified (DQ). And to be honest, I didn't know why! So, I asked my coach, and he said I did an extra stroke underwater that was not allowed. Darn!

Below is how I did for this competition:

- 50 back—improved 1.84 sec, placed 8th
- 50 breast—DQ :(
- 100 IM—improved 5.27 sec, placed 6th
- 50 free—improved .43 sec, placed 3rd
- 50 fly—58.62 seconds (my first time with this stroke), placed 5th

CHAPTER 2: BIG WEEKEND: TWO MEETS, TWELVE EVENTS

There were at least six swim clubs competing in this meet, so, hundreds of kids. I had a surprise at the event—a run-in with my friend from school, Clarke. Funny thing is that we were face-to-face and neither of us recognized each other. We both were wearing goggles and swim caps. Even with my mother in the stands gesturing like crazy at this boy, it did not clue me in as to why she was so excited. It was not until a few seconds later when his name was on the scoreboard that I realized I had known him for four years and was even in the same class for two of them! Funny how seeing him outside of school made him look different, so much so that we didn't recognize each other!

Swimming Is About Friends

I feel like I have been blessed. I have a great set of friends at my school (Clarence Center Elementary) which is the best school in the world. This is the part where I give a special shout-out to my friends: Camryn, Sam, Madison, Olivia, Hannah, and Julia. My principal is Ms. Coggins, and she is super nice. She runs a great school.

Also, I have another set of friends at my swim club BAAC (Buffalo Area Aquatics Club). Our coaches are Coach, Coach Tom, Coach Emma, Coach Aaron, and at times, Coach Jason, Coach Mike, and Coach Alyssa. Another shout-out to my bestie swim friends: Belle, Veronika, Lauren, Cara, Cadence, Celia, and Regan.

I have been part of a few different swim clubs/organizations: Clarence Learn to Swim, Park Club Sharks, BAAC, and Sanibel

SWAT (Sanibel Water Attack Team) program. We travel to Sanibel Island, Florida for vacation a couple of times a year. Sometimes, we stay for a week or two. When I am there, I want to do some practice sessions.

In Sanibel, I didn't know anyone there at first. But Coach Kurt made me feel comfortable, and I quickly made friends with Caroline, and soon it was just like being at home (only nicer weather). The pool is outdoors whereas I am used to swimming indoors. It does make a difference. Outdoors has more distractions like sounds, the sun, clouds, and other kids swimming in the Sanibel Recreation Department Pool. Sometimes after swim practice, Coach Kurt lets us slide down the big water slide!

Lucy practices at SWAT in Sanibel with Caroline

CHAPTER 2: BIG WEEKEND: TWO MEETS, TWELVE EVENTS

What I really like about swimming is seeing my friends and talking about everything from music to YouTube videos. As I mentioned, I really like a YouTuber/singer JoJo Siwa. My friends like her, too. We all like wearing the JoJo Bows. One of the things I sometimes convince my parents on is that if I beat my best time swimming in an event at a swim meet, I can get a new JoJo bow. I have nine so far!

I love YouTube. My parents think I spend far too much time watching it on my iPad. Luckily, I've had the chance to film at YouTube studios in New York City and in Toronto! My Dad is a nutritionist and exercise scientist; he does TV shows and video production in fitness & exercise, and he is also good friends with other TV personalities like Chef Binks and Matt Granite. Matt Granite is the Deal Guy on TV—he tests consumer products and recommends them for people to purchase.

Matt is always looking for a deal or a sale. When he needs kids to test kid's products on TV, he usually asks my dad, who then gets me to test the product and provide a review on camera. I first starting doing it when I was five, and I've done it dozens of times so far—it's so much fun!! Now, Luca and my sister, Serafina, have done it a few times, too.

YouTube New York was so much fun! We met Rachael Ray (cooking) and Ne-Yo (musician) while we were there. My Dad thought Ne-Yo was saying his name as Neil and kept calling him Neil, until finally, Ne-Yo said, "Not Neil, Ne-Yo." I was so embarrassed.

Luca and Lucy doing a toy commercial at YouTube Space Toronto

Chapter 3

BAAC In Action Open Meet

October 15, 2017

I was up early on Sunday morning. It was 5:30 AM—my dad was already in the kitchen on his laptop, drinking coffee. I was excited about the early event, but also tired from the day before. After 45 minutes of *Big Hero 6*, I ate breakfast and got ready for the meet.

We arrived at UB at 8 AM for warm-ups, and to our surprise, the meet officials asked my dad for help. They needed a few additional timekeepers to work the stopwatches and to verify the touchpad timers. It would be his first time on the pool deck during a meet. I was excited to see him down there with me, rather than in the stands.

I raced in many events that day—some went well, others worse. But then came the 100 free. I was off to a good start, and I thought I was moving at a good pace and had a good flip turn. Until I noticed a girl just a little in front of me when I was heading towards the finish. I tried to close the gap, but just wasn't able to catch her. I stretched far to touch the pads as quick as I could and then looked up at the scoreboard times. I had finished second. Good, but I had wanted to win.

Lucy waiting on deck for 100-Free Style BAAC meet

It wasn't until about 20 minutes later that my dad told me the good news. Although I did not win the heat of the event, I made a qualifying silver time! Which means I could compete for The Niagara Short Course Qualifier.

I now had one silver "qualifiers" time, and I was excited and determined to get more!

I had to wait two weeks until our TTSC Halloween Meet.

CHAPTER 3: BAAC IN ACTION OPEN MEET

Swimming Is About Improving

It would be great to drop time (swim faster) every time I swam, especially in meets. And I try— really hard. However, sometimes my time is worse (slower). My coaches tell me that this is natural and to not get discouraged. They remind us junior swimmers to keep working hard and improving, especially in practice.

I know not everyone loves practice. Sometimes it's long and tiring. However, my coaches do a good job of keeping it fun. We play sharks and minnows and rabbits, rats, and racoons. Sometimes they even let us play in the diving well or jump off the lowest of the high diving boards, not the platforms.

Private lessons:

Coach Ron & Coach Tom

I've worked with private coaches in addition to my swim team to help improve my technique. Coach Ron works with me outdoors in the summer while Coach Tom works with me indoors in the colder months, which living in Buffalo, is a lot.

My overall goal is to keep improving so that I get faster and faster. I would love it one day to swim in college. However, my number one goal would be to swim in the Olympics! My female swim idol is Katie Ledecky—she is amazing. I'd love to swim that fast someday. Also, I think Michael Phelps is wonderful. He's the best swimmer ever!

Coach Tom teaches Lucy on whiteboard during a private lesson

Chapter 4

TTSC Halloween Meet

October 27-29, 2017

This was my first time ever competing in a three-day meet. Usually, Friday night is reserved for the older kids, who can compete in longer races. However, my Mom decided to enter me into the 200 free.

I've never raced the 200 free before. In fact, the 100 free was the furthest I've ever raced in a meet up to this point. I've gone further than 200 free in practice before, but it's not the same thing. I was nervous that I wouldn't be able to keep up my speed for a full 200. Not to mention that I was also terrified I would come in last.

When the race began, I got off a little slow. My dives still need work; my coach has told me that my legs and feet come apart when I push off, which slows me down. I also know that

I need to use the strength from my legs to push off the block with more force. Regardless, I thought my streamline was good and that I was in decent shape for the rest of the race in the middle of the pack.

As the race went on, I started to feel a little tired. I tried to finish fast, but it's sometimes tough when you are out of breath. I also had lost count of the lap I was on (which, if you are a swimmer, you know it helps you keep pace). I was trying especially hard to make sure I did legal flip turns, and with my concentration elsewhere, I lost track of where I was in the pack. The good news is that sometimes not being in the lead is a good thing— it creates less stress and allows you to focus on your stroke. I noticed the girl to my left was a little in front of me, and I could tell it was near the end of the race, so I swam fast and reached for the wall. The race was over. I looked up. My time was 3:11.65. The time I need to beat was 3:18—I did it! Another B time! I wanted to make sure, so I asked the timer as well. She confirmed it. 3:11.65.

I was so excited! A qualifying B time in my first attempt at the 200 free! We left the pool that night, and I felt great! I couldn't wait to get back tomorrow for my next races.

I was still excited Saturday morning; I didn't feel anywhere near as nervous as Friday.

I raced in the 50 yard free and the 100 yard breaststroke. I got two more B times. I was swimming great! The only events of the day that I did not get B times in were the 50 butterfly and 100 backstroke. But I now had five of the six B times needed to move up in my practice group from bronze to silver.

CHAPTER 4: TTSC HALLOWEEN MEET

I had another chance on Sunday morning to challenge myself for qualifying B times. I was to race in the 50 backstroke and 50 breast. Both of these events gave me a good chance.

Now, on that Saturday night, I took a break from swimming and went to my friend Hannah's house for a fall party. There were 20 girls invited, most of them from my school. We did crafts like pumpkin decorating, made glitter slime, and even decorated canvas bags with our names on them. We also ate pizza, cupcakes, and drank apple cider. The last thing we did was decorate a candy apple.

Then the worst thing happened. In the middle of the night, my stomach started to hurt—bad. It woke me out of a deep sleep. I went to get my mom, and she got me a bucket. And I needed it—three times! I was so sick and felt awful.

I didn't think that I overate or had food poisoning. My mother confirmed that I had a stomach bug. Which meant she had to cancel my place at the meet on Sunday. I couldn't go! I knew I could have made one more B time, and now I'd have to wait at least two more weeks until the next swim event.

Swimming Is About Overcoming Disappointment

Sometimes disappointment is not swimming your best or not winning your event/heat. Sometimes it's not related to competition at all. Recently, our swim club changed our practice groups. I was in the "Age Group category" made up of mostly eight- and nine-year-olds. So, the older groups were as follows: Novice, Age Group (my group), Advanced Age group (better swimmers), and Seniors (the best swimmers).

My friends, Belle, Lauren, Veronika, Isabella, and Reagan, were in the same group as me. However, now I am in Bronze and Belle, Lauren, and Regan are in silver. The new groups are classified as: Novice, Bronze, Silver, Gold, and Senior. Being placed in the bronze group has caused me disappointment.

There are a lot of younger swimmers in my group—I am confused as to why I am not in Silver. Practice now seems too easy. I was used to swimming 200 yards, and now I am swimming only 25 yards for practice drills. I don't know why we only swim one-fourth of what silver swims. I'm not sure if this is because the younger swimmers cannot swim as far or as fast, but I am bored. We just swim one lap and then stop. My Mom and Dad are also worried that I will lose my conditioning and not be pushed towards new PRs (personal records).

I miss some of my friends, but worse than that, I feel like I should be with the faster swimmers. I really hope that I can make faster times in swim meets so that I can move back up to the better group. In the meantime, however, I just have to practice hard, do my best, and keep my head up.

Chapter 5

STAR Series Meet 2

November 11-12, 2017

The weekend of November 11th and 12th brought two swim meets. On Saturday November 11th, it was the Super Star Series Meet 2. I was so anxious to see if I could get my qualifying B time.

I was competing in three events for the day.

- 100 breast
- 100 back
- 100 free

I already had qualifying times in the 100 breast and the 100 free. So, the 100 back was my focus event.

The Star Series of swim meets are big events. Around ten teams are in attendance, which means a few hundred swimmers take part in the meet. What I enjoy most is racing against many swimmers, especially when you do not know them. It's exciting and sometimes intimidating to see all of the other swimmers and their times.

The Star Series meets are held in downtown Buffalo, NY at a place called Erie Community College (ECC for short), and the building is called The Flickinger Center. I love this pool—it's HUGE! But the water is cold (actually freezing—and I don't like it!)

The 100 back was the second event I swam in for the meet. I got off to a good start. As I pushed off the block, I tried to remember the instructions, "rotate your shoulders," that my stroke coach, Coach Tom, had taught me. I was almost halfway through the race and had to do my flip turn. I started too far away from the wall, and instead of having a powerful push off the wall, I felt like I drifted and lost speed. I swam as hard as I could towards the finish to try and catch up, but I didn't make it. I was still over three seconds too slow! I left the swim meet and the Flickinger Center disappointed.

The next morning, November 12th, was another meet, BAAC at It Again, at Buffalo State College. I was racing in five events:

- 50 yard back
- 100 yard IM
- 50 yard fly
- 50 yard breast
- 100 yard breast

CHAPTER 5: STAR SERIES MEET 2

This meet was much smaller—it was only inter club. I have noticed with myself that when a meet is smaller with less swimmers and less competition, I often swim slower. My Dad says that it could be from a lack of adrenaline and focus. I do often feel less nervous since I know most of the other swimmers.

Any of the events I was signed up for could have qualified for my final B time. Nevertheless, it still wasn't my best meet. I swam slower overall. By the end of the third event, I was already discouraged—all of my times were slower. Ugh!

Then came the 50 breast. I like the breast stroke. I only needed to beat 53.35 seconds to have a qualifying time. My previous best was 54.75 seconds. I finished with 53.15—I made it! My sixth B time!

I am now qualified to move up to the Silver group at the Buffalo Area Aquatic Club and practice with the better swimmers!

After the first two weeks of practice, I already loved swimming with the silver group! The practices are a little longer and definitely harder, but nothing I can't handle. I also feel like it's making me a better swimmer. I have also noticed that watching the techniques of other swimmers and learning from them is making me better as well. Now is the time to get even faster—Qualifiers are coming in February.

Swimming Is About Giving To Others

On Thursday December 21st, we had a Secret Santa exchange at swimming. I was the Secret Santa for my friend Reagan; she wanted a Ty Beanie Boo. My Secret Santa was Daphne. I wanted slime, candy, and Jo-Jo Bows (my favorite). But the Jo-Jo bows were over the $10 budget, so I just got the slime and candy, which was great! I know candy is unhealthy but my parents let me have candy once or twice per week. And I have been loving the slime!!

Giving to others is more than just giving holiday gifts. It's also about helping out when the situation calls for it. I have watched my friends give their towels, food, goggles, and bathing suits when others have forgotten or lost them. It's good to know that we look out for each other.

Chapter 6

BAAC to BAAC Open Meet

December 17, 2017

It was December 17th, 2017—BAAC to BAAC open meet at University of Buffalo. This is a meet presented by my swim club, Buffalo Area Aquatics Club (BAAC). When you arrive for a swim meet, you must check a registration sheet for your name. Under your name, you will see the events, heat, and lane that you will be in. Since we are in multiple events, we, as swimmers, are taught to write them on our hands.

On the morning of December 17th, I was in six events. I wrote the E/H/L on my hand and prepared for warm-ups.

When it was time for the first event, the 200 yard freestyle, I checked my hand and went to lane three. However, when it was time to step up to the starting block, the lane volunteer said that I was not in that lane, so I stepped down and started to panic.

Just then, another parent said I was in lane five, not lane three. I was in the wrong one since I couldn't read the writing on my hand! My writing was too sloppy. I hurried to lane five, but before I could take my starting position, they sounded the buzzer. The race began and I didn't make my start!

Originally, I was sad and didn't know what to do. Honestly, I thought I might cry, but then, one of my coaches had me report to the main starting official, and they put me into the next heat. I was relieved and even went on to swim a good race.

Swimming Is About Paying Attention To Details

I learned a lesson: to always be careful when writing the event/heat/lane on your hand. If you can't read your writing, like I couldn't, you might have trouble lining up correctly. Which can make you miss your race.

My parents tell me that the same thing happens at school. Sometimes I am not sure which assignment or book to bring home. Most of the time it's because I am talking to one of my friends or not paying attention to the teacher when she is talking. I need to remind myself to listen.

I realize now that the drama of missing my heat could have been avoided if I had taken the time to write neatly. I am pretty sure that it won't happen again. :)

Chapter 7

Star Series Meet 3

January 26-28, 2018

This was going to be a big weekend. Three days. Twelve events.

Swim clubs from both the Buffalo and Rochester, NY area of all ages. With hundreds of swimmers and thousands of spectators, the place was packed.

Luca, who is six, turning seven during the weekend of the event, is competing as well. He has been in a few meets before, but not many. He seems to like swimming but doesn't say much about it. I think he likes going to meets and hanging out with his swim friends, Matteo and Mason. Luca had events to swim in on Saturday and Sunday. On Friday night, Luca was with my Dad and younger sister, and they went out to Oak Stave for hamburgers. Why didn't they bring one home for me?

Friday, of a three-day swim meet, is when they do the longer races. I had the 200 freestyle. I am no longer afraid of the 200 free. However, this is a longer race in distance, so I knew it would take more energy. Also, I was somewhat sick—I had a runny nose and stuffiness most of the week. Not to mention my siblings were sick all week as well.

The water is cold at the Flickinger Center Pool, so I always brace myself for the first jump in the water. Would it be too much to ask for them to warm the water up a little? I thought I had a pretty good race—I had a good speed going, yet I didn't think it was my fastest. However, when it was over, I looked up and, sure enough, I beat my personal record. It was my best time for the 200 free, better than my previous by 0.92 seconds. It felt pretty good that I made a new personal record, even when I didn't feel like I was swimming my best. Maybe I was getting better?

Early Saturday morning, the place was packed. It seemed like there were even more swimmers than on Friday night. The sound system at the pool was blasting music—it's old-fashion music, like the stuff my mom listens to in the car, or what she used to listen to when she was 23. I wished they played more current tunes.

Before my first event of the day, the 50 yard breaststroke, which was event 17 of 63 for the day, my younger brother, Luca, was in event 16, the 25 yard breaststroke for boys 8 and under. As I mentioned, Luca has been in swim meets before, but not many. When it was time, Luca walked down to the starting blocks and found his assigned lane. I saw him talking to one of the lane timers who was checking her clipboard.

CHAPTER 7: STAR SERIES MEET 3

When the starters called all swimmers to the starting block to take their mark, Luca was not ready. He was still standing off to the side. The pool area was loud, and there were thousands of fans. I could see my mother waving her hands and screaming. The starter blew the whistle—all swimmers dove into the pool, but Luca was still standing on the pool deck. He missed his race!

Swimming Is About Being Helpful

Luca missed his race. I thought he might start to cry, but he didn't; in fact, he handled it pretty well. Over the next two days, he would have four more events, and I didn't want to watch him miss any more events. So, I took it upon myself to walk him down to the starting blocks. As I said, there are many teams and hundreds of swimmers. It's pretty easy to get confused when you have only swum in a few meets.

Although Luca is my younger brother and can be a little brat at times (and a big one too), I still wanted to see him swim well in the rest of his events. Swim teams are big, and sometimes the coaches need some help, especially with keeping track of the younger swimmers.

Serafina, Lucy and Luca at the Park Club before a swim meet - go Sharks!

Chapter 8

2018 BAAC Chance Open

February 11, 2018

This was a shorter event. It was at the pool at the University of Buffalo Alumni Area. This is the place where I practice four days a week. My "home turf or surf," if you will.

I was pretty excited to get some great times. I was hoping to shave off a few seconds from my 50 freestyle and 50 breaststroke and maybe even get my first gold time!

My events for the day were in this order:

- Event 4—100 yard breast
- Event 5—50 yard free
- Event 7—100 yard IM
- Event 9—50 yard back
- Event 14—100 yard back

- Event 15—50 yard breast

My brother and I arrived there at 8:00 AM for warm-ups—the meet began at 9 AM. It would be a long day with many swimmers and didn't finish until close to 2 PM.

Unfortunately, one by one, I kept gaining time. First in the 100 breast, then 50 free. I felt pretty good. I thought I was getting off to great starts and my turns, both flip and open turns, were improving. However, I proceeded to go through event by event and gain time in each.

By 2 PM, I looked at my times on Meet Mobile, the mobile app that records best times and current time, and I gained in all six events! This was the first time I had gotten slower in every event for the day. Although I was disappointed that I didn't have a great meet, I still felt pretty good. I liked my starts and I thought I swam well. Coach Tom told me afterwards that sometimes these things happen, and the best thing to do about it is to forget about it. Which I pretty much did by the time I got home and started watching Brooklyn and Bailey on YouTube.

Swimming Is About Overcoming Challenges And Bullying

Now that I am in the Silver practice group, practices can be pretty hard. Especially on Saturday mornings when the coaches work us the hardest. However, with more work comes more competition and fun, at least for most of us.

CHAPTER 8: 2018 BAAC CHANCE OPEN

On this one particular Saturday practice, there was a problem. One of the older swimmers in our group was being mean to the others.

In the pool, swimmers need to stay in their lanes. With the lanes, there are rules:

- Circle swimming—stay to the right side of the lane (which switches once you turn)
- Passing—if you need to pass a slower swimmer, do it quickly, and make sure you are faster than them. Don't speed up if someone touches your feet
- Etiquette—treat others with kindness and respect. Don't hurt anyone (kick on the way through)

This one swimmer was not treating others with kindness and respect. They were swimming over the top of others, kicking slower swimmers, and grabbing their legs to pull them back and slow them down. Sometimes even calling others inappropriate names. A few of my friends were victims to this bully that Saturday morning.

At first, they tried to ignore it, thinking that it was going to stop. However, that was not the case. So, they told the coach, who addressed it; the bad behavior continued, but to a lesser degree. When one of my friends got out of the water after practice, she immediately started crying. She was upset that another swimmer was bullying her.

Lucy on the starting blocks ready to dive

Thankfully, we have a great group of coaches, led by Coach Sam. They talked amongst themselves and have addressed the issues with that specific person. Bullying and being mean to one another is not acceptable. Swimming is about improving and having fun which cannot happen when you feel threatened or bullied. I am glad we have such great coaches and a club program that promotes fun and safe swimming. It truly is what makes me want to continue to swim and improve.

Chapter 9

2018 Niagara LSC Short Course Championship Qualifier

February 23-25, 2018

This was my first time in the Qualifiers, often called Silver. The event is normally for girls ten and under (I was nine at the time).

Friday:
- 200 free—dropped over 2.57 seconds (my best time ever)! Placed 20 of 25

Saturday:
- 50 breast—dropped 3.03. Placed 22 of 29
- 50 free—dropped 1.09. Placed 29 of 47

Sunday:
- 100 yard breast—gained 5.16 :(. Placed 32 of 33
- 100 yard free—dropped 5.92 seconds. Placed 22 of 35

On Friday, the first day of the meet, I am always the most nervous about not swimming well, coming in last, and about being embarrassed. My coaches tell me it's normal. My Dad says that being nervous is good—it means that it's important to you and you want to do well. I couldn't wait to start!

After going through warm-ups, I felt good and ready. The first dive into the water is the hardest. I jumped in and gave it all I had. The 200 free is a longer event—there is some strategy involved with pacing. My coaches are working with me on it, and I think I am getting better. I touched the pad at 3:04:09—my best time ever! It was my only event for the evening, and I felt like I got off to a great start!

I really do enjoy going to meets. I like seeing great swimmers and this meet, the Championship Qualifier, has the best swimmers in my age group and level from all over Western New York. Some were from faraway swim clubs and towns that I have never heard of. It's fun to meet new people and everyone is pretty friendly.

Saturday was a great day for me! I competed in two events: the 50 yard breast and 50 yard free. I dropped time in both and recorded my best time ever! I am convinced the Town of Tonawanda Pool is a faster pool than many others in the area. I usually have my best times there. Coach Tom says it's a deeper

CHAPTER 9: 2018 NIAGARA LSC SHORT COURSE CHAMPIONSHIP QUALIFIER

pool that has underwater currents that helps people swim faster. I don't know, but I like it!

Sunday was a different story. I started with the 100 yard breast as my first event. I was slow. I added over five seconds to my time. My Dad said it looked like I stopped and had a ham sandwich during the second half of the race. I felt sluggish. Maybe three days in a row was too much.

After the race, I had almost three hours before my next event. I ate my snack and sat next to my Dad. He tried to make me feel better. After I ate, we went through the program guide, the "heat sheets" as we call it, to see the other girls who would be racing in my next heat. Once I looked at the other seven girls, I realized that I knew most of them.

My Dad asked me if I was faster than them. I said YES. I knew I was. He said, "Then it's simple. Don't worry so much about your technique—just go out there and try to be faster than all the others." And that's exactly what I did. Which resulted in me dropping almost six seconds in my 100 yard free—my best time ever, and I won the heat! Swimming is about overcoming disappointment and doing your best!

Swimming Is About Great Exercise

I think swimming is a great form of exercise. I have been swimming for about five years now, and I know I am definitely stronger than when I started. My muscles sometimes get tired after long swimming practices, mostly my arms, shoulders, and legs.

My coaches have us do something called "dry land training" before we practice in the pool. Dry land training is mostly body weight exercises like push-ups, planks, lunges, squats, crunches, and jumps. Our coaches believe that working the muscles outside of the pool will make us stronger and better athletes in the pool.

In addition, my Dad works with me in his training center. His business mostly works with adults with their nutrition, fitness, physical rehabilitation, and health goals, but he helps me individually. Being in silver group, I don't have swim practice on Fridays, so my Dad picks me up from school or from home and brings me to his office.

I work with one of his trainers, but sometimes my Dad works with me himself. I've been doing pull-ups, planks, push-ups, and ball slams to help my upper body strength. I've also been doing squats, lunges, the farmer's walk, ball crunches, and stairs to work my legs and core. Recently, my Dad has been teaching me the movements of how to do a power clean—ughh. It's hard! But he tells me with a great form, my lower body, upper body, and core will help me get faster starts and have stronger strokes in the water.

He has always told me that exercise should be used as both performance and injury prevention (which he believes isn't emphasized enough). In other words, doing exercise helps prevent injuries that can happen from many hours of swimming, especially in the shoulders and back.

I like dry land training. Sometimes it's hard to do, but I think it will make me a better swimmer. Also, I think I just like spending time at my Dad's office!

CHAPTER 9: 2018 NIAGARA LSC SHORT COURSE CHAMPIONSHIP QUALIFIER

Lucy doing squats during her workout with her Dad

Food:

In addition to exercise training, my parents have always been promoting healthy eating for my family.

- Breakfast is oatmeal with protein powder or eggs
- Lunch is made and brought to school except on Fridays when we can buy school lunch

- Beverages are water except one small cup of almond milk in the morning
- Dinner is usually chicken and broccoli (I may soon begin to cluck)
- Desserts are limited to Sunday night, but sometimes Saturday if I have a great meet

What I like is that my mother packs me a snack after swim practice. So as we drive home at 8 PM from the University of Buffalo, I eat mixed nuts and whole grain crackers in the car. Sometimes I have protein powder and cottage cheese when I get home—I would love for it to be M&M's, but I know that won't help!

Sleep:

My parents have always had my brother, sister, and I follow a sleep routine. At times, my Dad will also pull the sleep data from my fitness tracker. He teaches classes on sleep quality in his business. He told me that, in addition to getting enough sleep, it's even more important to get quality sleep.

My dad describes it as the amount of time spent in deep sleep and less broken sleep cycles (sounds complicated, I know). Basically, when you are in deep sleep, the body repairs itself the quickest. This will help recover from swim practices, but also help with energy and attention in school. If I can get good grades and swim fast, I'm in!!

Chapter 10

Long Course Season

All of the swimming practices and meets that I have mentioned up until now have all been short course. In the United States, short courses are most common. A competitive pool is usually measured at 25 yards long. Normal high schools, swim clubs, and college swimming is usually short course.

However, we also have a shorter season called long course. In long course, the swimming lap is 50 meters long. Olympic swimming is done in LCM—long course meters.

Luckily, my swim team also gives us the opportunity to swim long course meters. At the University of Buffalo where I practice, the pool is set up to be both a long and short course pool. We are one of only three pools in the area that offer long course swimming.

Last year, when I was eight, I actually liked long course swimming better. I know that sounds weird because most people think that long course is harder since the laps are longer. However, last year, I wasn't that good at my flip and open turns. In fact, I was kind of scared to do them. So, with the long course, you do fewer of them. For the 50 meter free, back, breast, or butterfly, you don't have to do any turns!

This year, I'm not so sure. I am better at my two turns now. However, I still think the long course will work well for me. I feel like I have a lot of endurance and few turns should mean better times. I sure hope so!

Swimming Future

My goal right now is to keep swimming and continue to get better and faster. I want to swim in middle school and high school. My long-term goal is to swim in college—it would be so much fun to be on a college swim team and travel to other schools for a swim meet. Ultimately, I would love to swim in the Olympics!

I know it's early but I've already mapped out the Olympic schedule. Swimming is a summer Olympic Sport.

- 2020 Tokyo—I will only be 11 so unlikely
- 2024 Paris—I will be 15. Still unlikely but my mother wants to go to Paris
- 2028 Los Angeles—I will be 19 so fingers crossed
- 2032—not yet announced. I will be 24

CHAPTER 10: LONG COURSE SEASON

    I just started a swimgear store called Lucy Swimwear or BRB Swimwear (Lucyswimwear.com). I love to design, and I want to design swim caps, goggles, t-shirts, and bags. Maybe someday performance swim suits, both for practice and meets. I've always loved swimming gear. After the online store I'd love to eventually have a storefront somewhere on the beach!

    I think swimming is a great sport. Not only is it important to know how to swim as a safety skill, it's also a lot of fun, it's challenging, and you'll make the best friends. I would recommend swimming to anyone, especially kids who are looking for a sport they can really enjoy for a lifetime.

    Hope to see you in the 2028 Olympics, but in the meantime, BRB, I need to go to swim practice!

Love,

Luciana Alessi
BRB...I NEED to go to swim practice
♡ -Lucy ♡

Luciana (Lucy) Alessi
Lucyswimwear.com

Hey, looking for super cool and fun swimwear for kids and young adults?

Check out my store: **Lucyswimwear.com**

- Silicone Swim caps
- Tee-shirts
- Goggles

And more!

Contact management of this author:
info@lucyswimwear.com

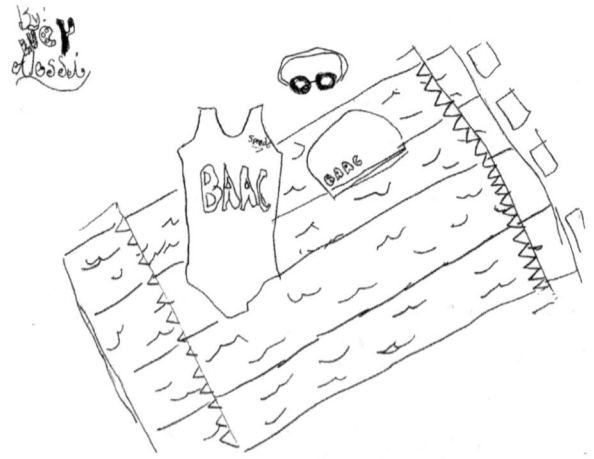

www.ingramcontent.com/pod-product-compliance
Lightning Source LLC
Chambersburg PA
CBHW052043070526
44584CB00018B/2583